Old M
Hubbard

A ZEBRA BOOK
Illustrated by Elizabeth Wood

PUBLISHED BY
WALKER BOOKS
LONDON

Old Mother Hubbard
Went to the cupboard,
To fetch her poor dog a bone;
But when she got there
The cupboard was bare
And so the poor dog had none.

She went to the baker's
To buy him some bread;
But when she came back
The poor dog was dead.

She went to the undertaker's
To buy him a coffin;
But when she came back
The poor dog was laughing.

She took a clean dish
To get him some tripe;
But when she came back
He was smoking a pipe.

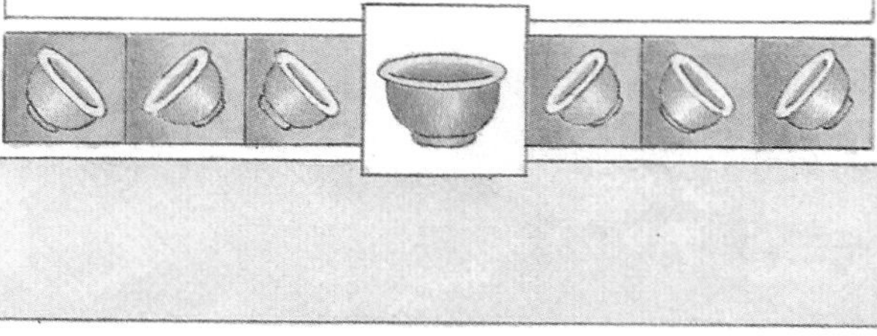

She went to the fishmonger's
To buy him some fish;
But when she came back
He was licking the dish.

She went to the fruiterer's
To buy him some fruit;
But when she came back
He was playing the flute.

She went to the tailor's
To buy him a coat;
But when she came back
He was riding a goat.

She went to the hatter's
To buy him a hat;
But when she came back
He was feeding the cat.

She went to the barber's
To buy him a wig;
But when she came back
He was dancing a jig.

She went to the cobbler's
To buy him some shoes;
But when she came back
He was reading the news.

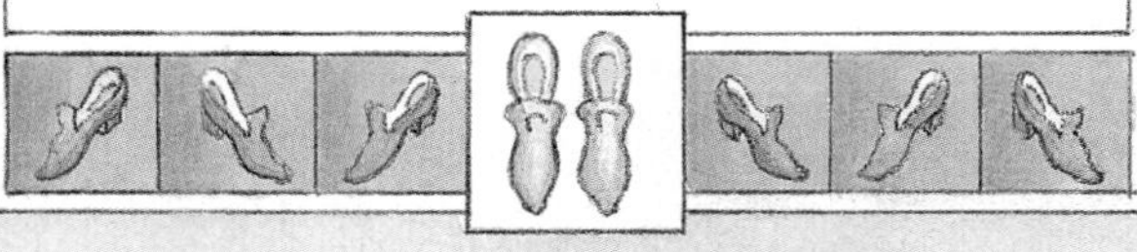

She went to the seamstress
To buy him some linen;
But when she came back
The dog was a-spinning.

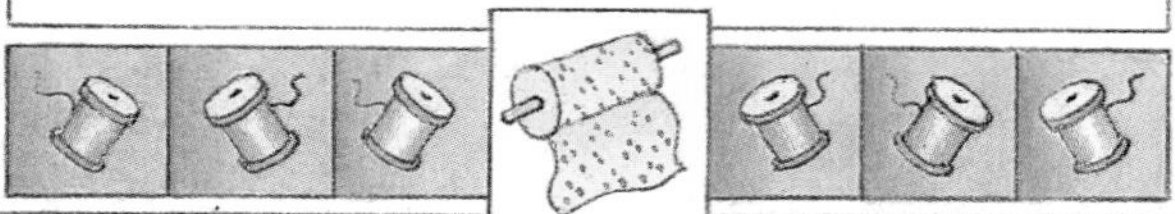

She went to the hosier's
To buy him some hose;
But when she came back
He was dressed in his clothes.

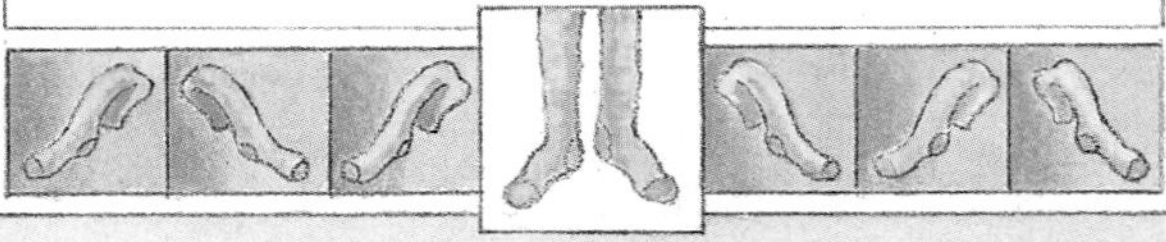

The dame made a curtsey,
The dog made a bow;
The dame said, Your servant,
The dog said, Bow-wow.